INTRODUCTION

Surinamese cuisine is a unique blend of different cultural influences, including indigenous, African, Asian, and Dutch. The country's diverse population has resulted in a rich and varied culinary tradition.
One of the most popular dishes in Suriname is Pom, a stew made with meat and vegetables. Another popular dish is Roti, a type of flatbread often filled with meat or vegetables. Moksi meti, a dish made with rice, beans, and meat, is also a staple in Surinamese cuisine.

Surinamese cuisine also features a variety of seafood dishes, such as Baka bana, which is made with fried banana and fish. Surinamese cuisine also includes a wide range of flavors from the different ethnic groups that make up the country.

The indigenous people of Suriname have influenced the cuisine with traditional ingredients such as cassava and wild game. African slaves brought their own culinary traditions, including dishes made with okra and plantains.

The Dutch, who colonized Suriname, have also had an impact on the cuisine, with dishes such as "erwtensoep" (pea soup) and "stamppot" (mashed potatoes with vegetables) being popular.

In addition to these traditional dishes, Surinamese cuisine has also been influenced by the Asian communities, particularly the Hindustani and Javanese. Dishes such as "nasi goreng" (fried rice) and "bami goreng" (stir-fried noodles) have become popular in Suriname.

Overall, Surinamese cuisine is a blend of various cultural influences, resulting in a rich and varied culinary tradition. With a mix of flavors and a wide range of ingredients, Surinamese cuisine is a delicious and satisfying experience for food lovers.

RECIPES

- 04 Pom
- 06 Bami
- 08 Nasi
- 10 Brown beans and rice
- 12 Saoto soup
- 14 Roti masala chicken
- 16 Stuffed Sopropo
- 18 Kwie Kwie
- 20 Braised bokking with rice or a bun
- 22 Nasi Kunig
- 24 Masala duck
- 26 Cassave soup
- 28 Pepre watra (Surinamese fish soup)
- 30 Peanut soup
- 32 Heri Heri
- 34 Bara
- 36 Gudangan
- 38 Pitjel
- 40 Okersoep Okro Bravoe
- 42 Stir-fried Tahoe
- 44 Long beans with salt meat
- 46 Prawns with coconut milk

1. POM

One of the most popular dishes in Suriname is "pom," a stew made with meat and vegetables. A comprehensive recipe for perfect pom, the holy grail of Surinamese cuisine.

Pom is a Surinamese oven dish made with the root vegetables of the tayer plant as the main ingredient. This plant grows in many parts of South America, including in the inland of Suriname.

Ingredients:

Chicken and salt meat filling

- 500 grams salt meat
- 1.2 kilograms chicken thighs
- 2 medium onions, finely chopped
- 4 cloves of garlic, minced
- 2 medium tomatoes, diced
- A few sprigs of celery, finely chopped
- 4 tablespoons butter
- 1 tablespoon allspice, nutmeg, and ground black pepper
- 2 teaspoons salt
- 75 milliliters olive oil
- 700 milliliters broth (made from two cubes)
- 4 tablespoons sugar
- 8 tablespoons ketchup
- 2 tablespoons sambal badjak (chili paste)

Pomtayer

- 2 kilograms pomtayer
- Juice of half a lemon
- 200 milliliters freshly squeezed orange juice (from about 2 large oranges)
- 6 tablespoons picalilly
- 2 tablespoons ground allspice
- 4 tablespoons white table sugar
- 4 tablespoons ketchup
- 1 teaspoon salt
- 1 Maggi bouillon cube, dissolved in 200 milliliters water
- Half a bunch of celery, finely chopped
- 3 tablespoons butter

Instructions:

Step 1: Prepare the chicken and salt meat filling
1. Cook the salt meat in a large pot of water for 15 minutes, then rinse and cut into small cubes. Set aside.
2. Finely chop the onion, garlic, celery, and tomato.
3. In a soup pan, melt butter and sauté the onion and garlic. Add the tomato, celery, and salt meat cubes and simmer for 10 minutes.
4. Prepare the chicken by washing it and cutting it into thin, flat pieces. Mix together the allspice, nutmeg, pepper and salt and rub it on the chicken.
5. In a skillet, heat olive oil and brown the chicken on both sides for 1-2 minutes. Remove the chicken from the skillet and deglaze the pan with 100ml of broth.
6. Add the chicken, salt-meat-tomato mixture, remaining broth, ketchup, and sugar to the pan and simmer for 10 minutes.
7. Strain the chicken and vegetables out of the pan, leaving behind a red-colored gravy. If desired, add sambal to the gravy and cook for an additional 10 minutes, stirring frequently, to thicken and intensify the flavor.
8. Set the chicken and gravy aside until the pomtayer base is ready.

For the pomtayer:
1. Preheat the oven to 175 degrees.
2. Remove the pomtayer from the package and add the "sour" ingredients (picalilli, lemon juice and orange juice) to prevent discoloration. Stir well.
3. Add the allspice, sugar, ketchup, salt, broth, and a large handful of chopped celery to the pomtayer base, then add 75ml of the gravy from the chicken.
4. Taste the pomtayer and adjust the seasoning as needed with salt, black pepper, lemon, or a crumbled stock cube.

Preparing the pomtayer in the oven:
1. Grease a baking dish generously with butter, including the edges of the dish.
2. Spread a layer of 1.5-2 cm of the pomtayer mixture in the baking dish, using a spatula to evenly distribute it.
3. Place the large pieces of chicken on top of the pomtayer layer, covering it as much as possible.
4. Spread the salt meat, onion, tomato, and garlic mixture between the chicken pieces.
5. Spread the remaining pomtayer mixture on top of the chicken and salt meat layer, and smooth it out.
6. Pour the gravy over the top of the pomtayer, using a small gravy spoon or tablespoon to spread it evenly.
7. Bake the dish in the oven at 175 degrees for 1 hour and 45 minutes. Turn the dish over after 50 minutes to ensure even cooking. Check the pomtayer by pricking it with a fork, if it comes out clean then it is ready.
8. Let the pomtayer cool before cutting into it, as it will taste best if left to rest for at least a day before eating.

MY NOTES

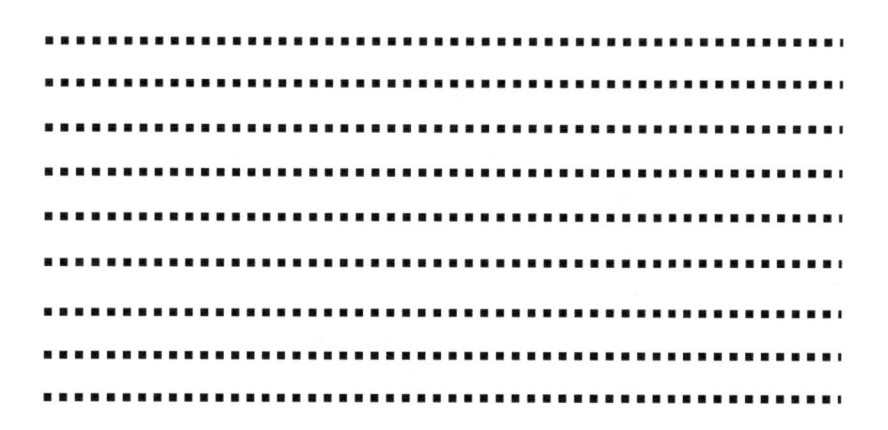

....
....
....
....
....
....
....
....
....

2. BAMI

Bami goreng is a well-known and popular dish in Suriname, it is a type of fried noodle dish that is typically made with a combination of ingredients like vegetables, meat or seafood. The dish is usually served with a spicy sauce and it is believed to have originated in China but has been adapted to include local flavors and ingredients. Bami is one of the most common street foods in Suriname.

Surinamese cuisine is a unique blend of various cultural influences, due in part to the diverse population of the country. The Javanese immigrants played a big role in creating dishes like Bami, however it is not a true Surinamese dish. The mixture of Hindu, Creole, Javanese, Chinese, and other ethnic groups has greatly impacted the way food is prepared in Suriname. Traditional dishes like Nasi Goreng, Soto Ajam, and Bami Goreng have been adapted to the local palate, resulting in a wide range of authentic and flavorful dishes. The cuisine is true to its roots and not adulterated with foreign elements.

Ingredients:

- 500 grams spaghetti
- 3 small square Maggi cubes
- 1 onion, finely chopped
- 2 cloves of garlic, minced
- 300 grams chicken thigh fillet, cut into bite-size pieces
- 4 sprigs of fresh celery, finely chopped
- Sunflower oil, for frying
- 1/2 teaspoon black pepper
- 1/2 teaspoon 5 spice powder
- 1 piece of fresh ginger, 2 centimeters long and grated
- 1 teaspoon tomato paste
- 5 teaspoons salty soy sauce
- 2 teaspoons sweet soy sauce

Instructions:

1. Cook spaghetti in a large pot of boiling water with 2 Maggi cubes until al dente.
2. While the spaghetti cooks, finely chop the garlic and onion and cut the chicken thigh fillets into pieces. Coarsely chop the celery leaves.
3. Drain the cooked spaghetti and return it to the pot. Add ½ tablespoon of sunflower oil, 1 tablespoon of salt, and 1 tablespoon of sweet soy sauce, and mix well.
4. Heat a large wok over medium-high heat and add 1 tablespoon of sunflower oil. Sauté the onion and garlic for 1 minute.
5. Add 1 Maggi cube, black pepper, 5-spice powder, ginger, and a splash of water, and fry for another 2 minutes.
6. Add the chicken pieces and fry until browned on the outside and cooked through. Fry the tomato paste for another minute.
7. Reduce the heat and add 4 tablespoons of salted and 1 tablespoon of sweet soy sauce, and gently mix in the spaghetti. Warm through and taste for seasoning, adding more salt or sweet soy sauce as needed.
8. Lastly, add the chopped celery and mix well. Serve hot.

MY NOTES

3. NASI

Nasi goreng, a traditional dish from Indonesia, has many variations circulating. One such variation is the Surinamese version, which was created by Javanese immigrants who introduced the dish to Suriname and adapted it to include local spices.

Nasi, also known as rice dishes, are a staple in Surinamese cuisine. It is a popular one-pot meal that is often served with various accompaniments such as meat or fish dishes, vegetables, and sambals (spicy condiments). The rice is typically cooked with a variety of herbs and spices, such as curry powder, cumin, and coriander, which give it a unique and flavorful taste.

Surinamese nasi is similar to traditional Indonesian nasi dishes, as Suriname was a Dutch colony and many Indonesian people were brought over as contract workers. The influences of different cultures like the Javanese, Chinese and Indian can be found in Surinamese cuisine, and in the nasi dishes in particular.
There are many variations of Surinamese nasi, but the most popular one is nasi goreng, which is a fried rice dish. It is made by stir-frying cooked rice with a mixture of spices, vegetables, and meat or seafood. The rice is often flavored with soy sauce, kecap manis (sweet soy sauce), and sambal (chili paste) for a savory and slightly spicy taste.

Overall, Surinamese nasi is a delicious and versatile dish that can be enjoyed with a variety of different accompaniments, making it a perfect meal for any occasion.

Ingredients:

- 500gr basmati rice
- 1 large onion
- 6-8 cloves of garlic
- 2-4 maggi cubes
- 1 small piece of trassie (no more than the size of a 10ct coin)
- 1ts black pepper
- 1/2tl allspice powder
- 2cm fresh ginger chopped into 2 pieces
- 1 chicken breast
- 50gr/small bowl of dried shrimps
- sweet soy sauce
- salt ketjap/chinese black soy
- 3 stalks of celery (just the leaves)
- 100gr peas (frozen is fine)
- sunflower oil

Instructions:

1. Cook the rice according to package instructions and let it cool.
2. Soak dried shrimp in a bowl of water for 30 minutes.
3. There are two ways to prepare the chicken:
   - Method 1: Cook the chicken in water with a stock cube and sprig of celery. Once cooked, let it cool and fluff or cut it into small pieces.
   - Method 2: Marinate the chicken in crumbled maggi cube for an hour in the refrigerator. Fry it in oil until cooked and crispy. Let it cool and fluff it.
4. Finely chop the onion, garlic, and celery leaves. Set the celery leaves aside for later.
5. In a wok, heat some sunflower oil and fry the onion and garlic mixture. After 2 minutes, add the black pepper, allspice powder, ginger, 2 maggi cubes and trassie. Add a small splash of water to make a paste. Fry for a few minutes.
6. Add the chicken and shrimp. Fry for another 1-2 minutes. Add the peas and cook for another minute.
7. Turn down the heat and add half the rice. Add 4 tablespoons of salted soy sauce and 2 tablespoons of sweet soy sauce. Stir well for a few minutes until the rice is browned.
8. Add the remaining rice, 3 tablespoons of salted soy sauce, and 1 tablespoon of sweet soy sauce. Stir well until the rice is browned.
9. Stir in the celery leaves.
10. Fried rice can be served with various accompaniments such as chicken satay, cucumber pickles, Surinamese chicken, stir-fried string beans with garlic and onion, or stir-fried spinach and thin strips of omelette.

MY NOTES

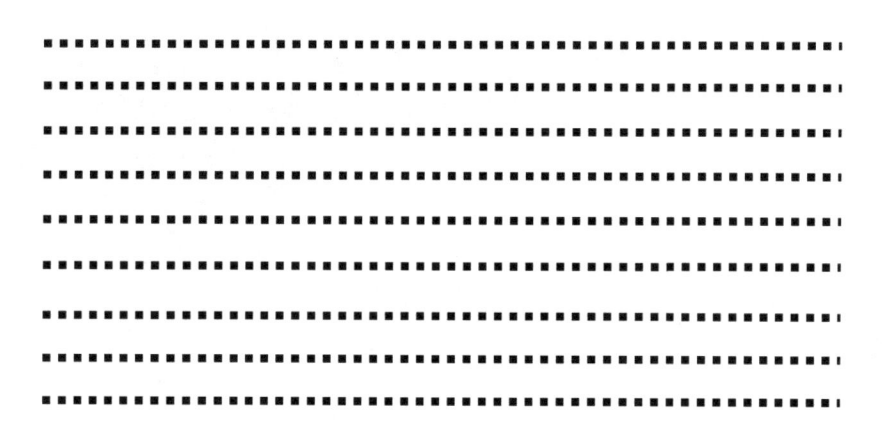

4. BROWN BEANS WITH RICE

Surinamese brown beans with white rice is a traditional and popular dish in Surinamese cuisine. It is a simple yet flavorful dish that is typically made with brown beans that are cooked with various herbs and spices, such as garlic, cumin, and cilantro, and served over a bed of white rice.
The beans are often cooked in a pressure cooker or Dutch oven until they are tender. Then the beans are seasoned with onion, garlic, and other spices. The beans are then served over a bed of white rice, which is typically cooked with a small amount of oil and salt.

The dish is often served with a variety of accompaniments, such as fried plantains, a fried egg, or a spicy sambal, which can be added to the dish to give it a kick of heat. It can also be served with a variety of meats such as chicken, fish or beef.
The dish is considered a comfort food for many Surinamese, it is also a very popular dish among the Afro-Surinamese and Creole communities in Suriname. The dish is also a staple in the Caribbean and South American countries and it is often referred to as "rice and beans".

Overall, Surinamese brown beans with white rice is a simple and satisfying dish that is packed with flavor, making it a perfect meal for any occasion.

Ingredients:

- 1/2 medium onion, finely chopped
- 1 garlic clove, minced
- 1 tomato, diced
- 250 grams smoked sausage
- 720 grams pot brown beans
- 2 teaspoons sugar
- Pinch of salt
- 6 allspice grains
- 3 sprigs of soup vegetables
- 1/2 4-gram stock cube
- Pinch of nutmeg
- Optional: Mme Jeannette pepper
- Optional: Salt meat (small diced)

Instructions:

1. Dice the tomato and chop the onion.
2. In a pan, heat 1 tablespoon of oil and fry the onions until translucent. Add the garlic and fry for another 30 seconds.
3. Add the diced tomatoes to the pan and fry until softened.
4. (Optional) Soak the salt meat in a bowl of water for 5 minutes, then cut it into small pieces. Fry it in the pan.
5. Add the entire contents of the pot of brown beans, including sugar, salt, soup vegetables, allspice grains, stock cube, and nutmeg.
6. Cut the sausage into small pieces and add it to the pan.
7. Fill the empty pot of brown beans with water and add it to the pan.
8. Let the mixture simmer on low heat for about 30 minutes or until the brown beans are cooked through and tender.
9. (Optional) Add a Madam Jeannette pepper for aroma, and let it simmer for the last 10 minutes. If you want the dish to be spicy, pierce the pepper before adding it to the beans.

Note: Madam Jeannette pepper is a type of chili pepper that is commonly used in Surinamese cuisine, but if it is not available, you can use any other kind of chili pepper you have.

MY NOTES

5. SAOTO SOUP

Surinamese Saoto soup is a traditional and popular dish in Surinamese cuisine. It is a spicy and flavorful soup that is typically made with a variety of herbs and spices, such as cumin, coriander, and lemongrass, and served with rice cakes and fried noodles.

The soup is often made with a variety of meats such as chicken, beef or mutton, and vegetables, such as potatoes, carrots, and cabbage. It is flavored with a variety of herbs and spices, such as cumin, coriander, and lemongrass, which give it a unique and aromatic taste. Some saoto soup recipes also contain peanuts, which add an extra crunchy texture. The soup is typically served with rice cakes, which are made from glutinous rice flour, and fried noodles, which are made from wheat flour. The rice cakes and fried noodles are often added to the soup and cooked in the broth for a short time before serving.
Saoto soup is considered as a comfort food for many Surinamese people. It is a popular street food and it is often sold by street vendors, it is also a common dish found in restaurants and homes.

The soup is also popular in other countries in the region such as Indonesia and the Netherlands, where it has been introduced by the Indo-Surinamese community.

Overall, Surinamese Saoto soup is a delicious and flavorful dish that is packed with a variety of herbs and spices, and is typically served with rice cakes and fried noodles, making it a perfect meal for any occasion.

Ingredients:

- 3 liters of water
- 600 grams soup chicken (preferably legs)
- 4 centimeters of laos (galangal)
- 4 cloves of garlic, left whole
- 1 onion, peeled and cut in half vertically
- 1 sprig of lemon grass (sereh)
- 1 salam leaf
- 2 large stock cubes
- 1 teaspoon herb bouillon
- 1 teaspoon white pepper

Note: Laos (galangal) is a root similar to ginger, it's common in Southeast Asian cuisine and it's often used in Surinamese cuisine as well. If it's not available, ginger can be used as a substitute. The salam leaf is a type of bay leaf that is commonly used in Indonesian and Surinamese cuisine, but if it's not available, you can use bay leaf instead.

Ingredients for garnish:

- 6 boiled eggs
- 300 grams bean sprouts
- 2 packets of fried potato sticks (julien)
- 1 packet of fried vermicelli (soe-on)
- Fried onions
- 2 double chicken fillets, filleted
- 1 sprig of celery, finely chopped
- 1 pepper, diced
- 5 tablespoons salted soy sauce

Note: Julien are thin and crispy potato sticks which are commonly used as garnish in Surinamese cuisine. Soe-on is a type of fried vermicelli that is commonly used as a garnish in Surinamese cuisine.

Instructions:

1. Cut the soup chicken into 3 or 4 large pieces and wash it thoroughly. Bring 3 liters of water to a boil in a large pot.
2. Add the chicken, laos, garlic, onion, lemon grass, 1 salam leaf, bouillon cubes, and white pepper to the boiling water. Bring it to a boil and then let it simmer for 30 minutes.
3. Remove the chicken breast from the pot and let the soup continue to cook on low heat for 1 hour. Taste the soup and add more salt or bouillon cubes if needed.
4. While the soup is cooking, fillet the chicken breast, boil the eggs, and peel them. Clean the bean sprouts and fry the soe-on (vermicelli) or prepare them as desired.
5. Once all the ingredients are ready, put them in separate bowls. Remove the seeds from the pepper and mix it with 5 tablespoons of salted soy sauce to make the soy sauce sambal.
6. To serve, place a boiled egg, bean sprouts, fried potato sticks (julien), a little fried onions, the filleted chicken breast, and vermicelli in a soup bowl. Pour the soup over the ingredients and garnish with celery.
7. Add a spoonful of the soy sauce sambal for extra flavor and spiciness if desired.

MY NOTES

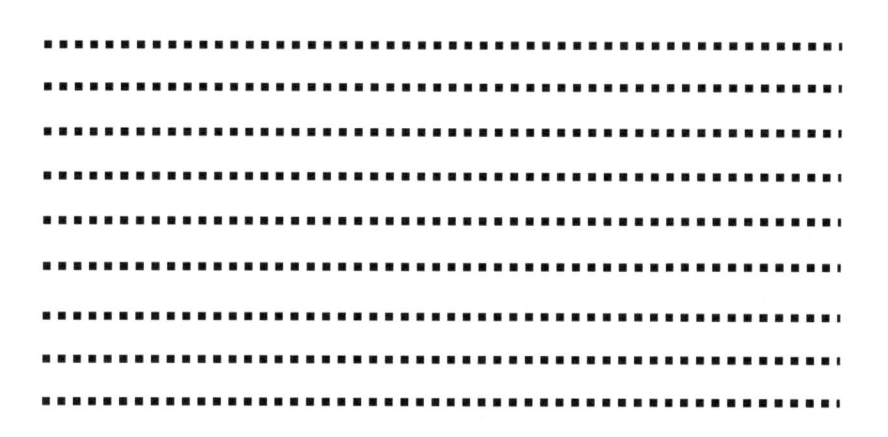

6. ROTI MASALA CHICKEN

Roti is a traditional dish that originated from the Indian subcontinent and has become popular in Surinamese and Dutch cuisine. It is often enjoyed as a staple dish, particularly in the form of a "massala and roti plate" which is a combination of meat or vegetable curry with a roti bread.

Roti can be prepared in a variety of ways, depending on the recipe or personal preference. Some popular methods include using ghee or butter to fry the dough, adding different spices to the dough or using different types of flour to make the dough.
It is a versatile dish that can be filled with a variety of meats and vegetables such as chicken, lamb, potato, or chickpea filling. Roti is often served with different curries and chutneys, making it a delicious and satisfying meal.

Roti is enjoyed by many people in Suriname and Netherlands, it is a popular street food and it is often sold by street vendors, it is also a common dish found in restaurants and homes.

Overall, Roti is a tasty and versatile dish that can be prepared in various ways and enjoyed with a variety of toppings and sides, making it a perfect meal for any occasion.

Ingredients:

- 800g chicken drumsticks
- 1 onion, shredded
- 2 cloves of garlic, pressed
- 1.5 tbsp massala spice
- 1 tsp tomato paste
- 1 cup water
- 1.5 tbsp garden herb broth (or 3 Maggi cubes)
- Pinch of black or white pepper
- 4 tbsp sunflower oil

Ingredients for the long beans and potato:

- 400g long beans, cut into 2-inch pieces
- 6 large potatoes, cut into large cubes
- 1 clove garlic, pressed
- 1 tbsp herb broth (2 Maggi cubes)
- 1 small onion, shredded
- 1 tbsp massala spice
- 1 tsp tomato paste
- 1 cup water
- Pinch of black or white pepper
- 6 eggs (optional)

Instruction:

1. Cut the chicken legs into desired pieces and wash them.
2. Heat oil in a large pan and sauté onions and garlic until they are translucent.
3. Add the tomato paste, massala and black/white pepper and stir well.
4. Add the chicken and stir.
5. Add the herb broth or Maggi cubes, cover the pan and let it cook for 5 minutes.
6. Add half a cup of water and continue to cook until the chicken is tender. This should take about 30 minutes.
7. Check for gravy and add the remaining water if needed. Taste for salt and adjust as necessary.

Instructions potatoes:

1. Heat oil in a pan and sauté onions and garlic until they are translucent.
2. Add the tomato paste, massala powder and stir well.
3. Add the diced potatoes, herb broth (maggi cubes), and a cup of water.
4. Cook on low flame, stirring occasionally, until the potatoes are almost done.
5. Add the long beans, stir well and cook until they are tender.
6. Taste for salt and adjust as necessary by adding more herb broth (1 maggi cube).
7. While the potatoes and long beans are cooking, prepare hard-boiled eggs.
8. Once the eggs are peeled, place them in the massala for a few minutes to coat them and make them yellow.
9. Serve and enjoy your meal.

MY NOTES

....
....
....
....
....
....
....
....
....

7. STUFFED SOPROPO

Sopropo, also known as Momordica charantia or balsam pear, is a vegetable that is commonly grown in Suriname. The vegetable is a popular ingredient in Surinamese cuisine, where it is often used in a variety of dishes.

In Suriname, sopropo is typically prepared by peeling and removing the seeds from the fruit before cooking. It is then used in dishes such as stews, curries, and soups. Sopropo is also commonly eaten raw and is often used as a side dish, accompanied with a spicy sauce.
Sopropo is also used in traditional Surinamese medicine, where it is believed to have medicinal properties that can help with various health issues such as diabetes, high blood pressure, and constipation.

The fruit is also known for its slightly bitter taste, which is often balanced out with other ingredients such as coconut milk, spices and hot peppers. Some Surinamese people use it in combination with other ingredients to make a dish called "pom". This dish is a stew that is made from sopropo, chicken, and other vegetables.

In Suriname, Sopropo is also known as "peerkanker" which means "pear cancer" or "pear sickness". This is because of the shape of the fruit and the bitterness.

Overall, Sopropo is an important ingredient in Surinamese cuisine and culture, and it's used in various ways to prepare delicious and healthy dishes, as well as traditional medicine.

Ingredients:

- 3 sopropos (Momordica charantia)
- 250 grams minced meat
- 1 large onion, finely chopped
- 3 tomatoes, diced or 1 tablespoon tomato paste
- 2 cloves of garlic, minced
- 1 tablespoon turmeric powder or 2 bouillon cubes
- A pinch of white or black pepper
- 2 tablespoons sugar
- 2 cups of oil for frying
- 1 1/2 cups of water
- 1 beaten egg
- 2 slices of bread or 3 crumbled rusk.

Instructions:

1. Begin by cutting off the tops of the sopropos and then using a spoon to hollow out the inside, discarding the seeds. Cut the sopropos into 10 cm pieces.
2. Make small slices in the sopropos with a knife and wash them with a mixture of water and salt.
3. In a separate bowl, mix together the minced meat, half of the chopped onion, the beaten egg, bread or crumbled rusk, white pepper, one minced garlic clove, and half a tablespoon of herbs. Use this mixture to stuff the sopropos and, if there is any leftover, shape it into small meatballs.
4. Heat a pan with 1.5 cups of oil and fry the stuffed sopropos until they are golden brown.
5. To make the sauce, heat another pan with 1 tablespoon of oil and add the remaining chopped onion, one minced garlic clove, diced tomatoes or tomato paste, and the remaining herbs. Allow the mixture to simmer and then add water and sugar.
6. Add the fried sopropos to the sauce and let it braise until the sopropos are tender. Serve with rice.

MY NOTES

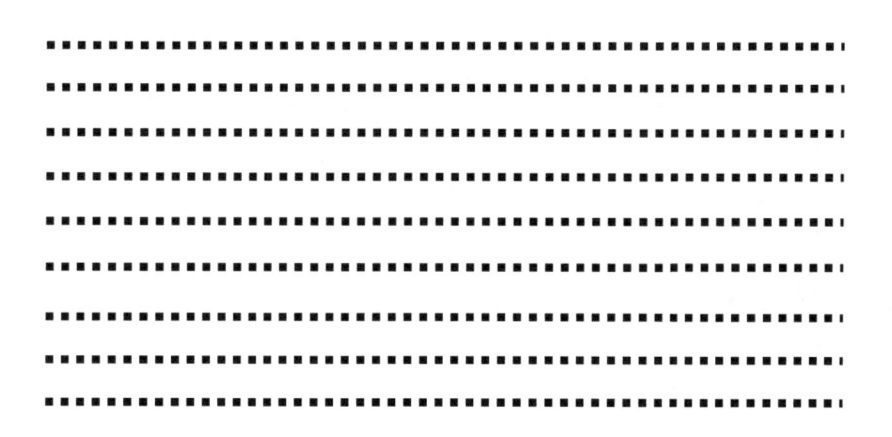

....
....
....
....
....
....
....
....
....

8. KWIE KWIE

Kwie Kwie is a delicacy among Surinamese fish dishes. It's an armored freshwater fish that is often prepared in a masala or curry. In the Netherlands, Kwie Kwie can be difficult to find fresh, and can typically only be found frozen at specialty markets.

The fish is typically caught in rivers, creeks and ponds in Suriname and is known for its unique flavor and texture. It has a firm white flesh and a mild taste. It is commonly used in traditional Surinamese dishes such as Kwie Kwie masala and Kwie Kwie with roti, a type of Indian flatbread.

In Suriname, Kwie Kwie is often cooked with a variety of spices such as cumin, turmeric and coriander, and combined with other ingredients such as onions, tomatoes, and hot peppers to make a flavorful curry.

In The Netherlands and other countries, Kwie Kwie is not as common, and it's difficult to find it fresh. It's only available in the frozen form in the tokos or specialty markets.

Overall, Kwie Kwie is a unique and delicious fish that is an important part of Surinamese cuisine and culture. It's a must-try for those who are looking to experience the diverse flavors of Surinamese food.

Ingredients:

- 8 fresh or frozen Kwie Kwie fish
- 1 large onion, finely chopped
- 3 cloves of garlic, minced
- 2 tomatoes, diced
- 2 teaspoons of tomato paste
- 3 tablespoons of masala spice blend
- 1 Madam Jeanette pepper
- 1 Maggi cube or 2 teaspoons of herb stock
- 1 can of coconut milk
- 3 vegetables (such as carrots, potatoes, and celery)
- 1 cup of water
- Salt, to taste
- Oil for cooking

Please note that depending on the recipe, different ingredients might be used, but this list is a good start for a Kwie Kwie Masala.

instructions:

1. Clean and gut the fish, leaving them whole and do not remove the head. Fry the fish in oil until half-cooked.
2. Remove the seeds from the pepper and chop it into small pieces. Chop the onions and garlic and combine them with the masala and a pinch of salt.
3. In a wok or pan, heat 4-6 tablespoons of oil and fry the masala mixture until it is nicely browned. Remove the core and seeds from the tomatoes and chop them into small pieces.
4. Add the tomatoes, tomato paste, and Maggi cube or herb stock to the masala and stir for about 2 minutes.
5. Add the fish to the masala and pour in 1 cup of water. Cover the pan and simmer over low heat for 25-30 minutes.
6. 5 minutes before turning off the heat, add a can of coconut milk and adjust the seasoning with Maggi cube, herb stock, or salt to taste.
7. Once the heat is turned off, sprinkle finely chopped vegetables over the fish and serve with rice and a side of Surinamese vegetables.

Tips: You can also add potatoes or young ochros to the Kwie Kwie or add a touch of acidity by adding green mango to this recipe.

MY NOTES

9. BRAISED BOKKING WITH RICE OR A BUN

Bokking is a type of smoked fish that is popular in Suriname. It is made from various types of fish such as mullet, catfish, or tilapia. It is often marinated in a mixture of spices and then smoked over a wood fire. The resulting fish is a dark brown color, and has a strong smoky flavor. Bokking is often served as a side dish or in sandwiches. It is also used in traditional Surinamese dishes such as roti with bokking and bokking in a spicy sauce. Bokking is not only popular in Suriname but also in the Caribbean.

Bokking is a traditional Surinamese and Caribbean dish that has been enjoyed for centuries. It can be found with or without the innards, such as roe. I prefer the filleted version, which can be found vacuum packed in the refrigerated section of supermarkets or tropical stores.

There are many ways to prepare bokking, but I have chosen to show a simple recipe for stewed bokking with rice or as a sandwich filling. Bokking is an inexpensive and long-lasting food that was traditionally consumed due to the lack of facilities to keep food fresh.

Ingredients:

- 1 large, fatty smoked bokking
- 3 teaspoons of oil
- 1 large onion, finely chopped
- 1 tomato, diced or 1 teaspoon of tomato paste
- 3 cloves of garlic, minced
- Salt and pepper, to taste
- 1 fresh pepper, chopped
- 1 tablespoon of sugar
- 1/2 cup of water

Note: Depending on the recipe, different ingredients might be used, but this list is a good starting point for a simple Bokking stew.

Instructions:

1. Clean the bokking by removing the skin, spine, bones, and head. Cut the fish into pieces, not too small, so it does not fall apart. Soak the fish in water and rinse it at least 2 times to desalt it. You can also add a little lemon juice to the last rinse to reduce the fishy smell.
2. Chop the onion and garlic and dice the tomatoes.
3. Heat a pan with the oil and fry the onion and garlic in it. If you are using pepper, add it after about 2 minutes. Stir in 1 tablespoon of brown sugar. Then add the tomatoes or tomato paste, and fry for a few more minutes, stirring well to prevent burning.
4. Add the bokking to the pan and pour in a little water. Cover the pan and let it steam on medium heat. Bokking is a cooked fish, so it will not take long to cook.
5. After a few minutes, remove the lid, and when the liquid has thickened a bit, the bokking is almost ready. Leave the lid off and let simmer for a few more minutes. Sprinkle salt and pepper to taste and finely chop a sprig of soup vegetables (celery) and garnish the bokking with them.

Tips: Serve braised bokking with white rice, a Surinamese tip or boiled or fried cassava. To make it a little fresher, you can sauté in pieces of green mango.

MY NOTES

10. NASI KUNIG

Nasi Kuning is a traditional Indonesian dish made with yellow rice brought to Surinam by Javanese immigrants. The rice is colored yellow using turmeric powder, which gives it its characteristic color and a subtle earthy flavor. The rice is typically steamed, but in some variations, it can be cooked by boiling or baking.

The dish is often served with various side dishes such as meat or fish curry, vegetables, and sambal (a chili paste condiment). It is also often garnished with fried shallots, chopped scallions, and sometimes a fried egg.
Nasi Kuning is a staple in Indonesian cuisine, and it's often served in special occasions such as weddings, religious ceremonies, and festivals. It's also often sold in street food stalls, warungs (small eateries) and traditional markets.

In addition to its delicious taste, turmeric, a key ingredient in Nasi Kuning, is known for its numerous health benefits such as its anti-inflammatory properties and its ability to improve brain function.

Nasi Kuning is a must-try for those who are interested in experiencing the rich and diverse flavors of Indonesian cuisine.

Ingredients:

- 250 grams of rice
- 1 large onion, finely chopped
- 4 cloves of garlic, minced
- 25 grams of laos, finely chopped
- 2 salaam leaves
- 1/2 teaspoon ground cumin seeds (briefly toasted in a pan)
- 1/2 teaspoon ground coriander seeds (briefly toasted in a pan, cumin and coriander seeds can be toasted together in a pan)
- 1/2 tablespoon sugar
- 15 grams trassi
- 2 stock cubes
- 1 can of coconut milk (400 ml)
- 1/2 teaspoon kunjite (turmeric powder)
- Salt to taste
- 3 tablespoons oil

Note: Depending on the recipe, different ingredients might be used, but this list is a good starting point for Nasi Kuning.

Instructions:

1. Put the onion, garlic, laos, kunjite, trassi, stock cube, sugar, coriander, and cumin in a food processor and grind it finely.
2. Heat a pan with oil and fry the ground spices, stirring for a moment until it comes to taste.
3. Then add the coconut milk and salaam leaves and let it cook. Then add the rice and stir.
4. Then add water up to your second knuckle and stir again, let it cook until the water is almost evaporated.
5. Option 1: Put on low heat and close it with a lid for a few minutes until the rice is cooked. Turn the rice occasionally and close it again and turn off the heat.
6. Option 2: Or, when the water is almost evaporated, put it in a steamer and steam it until cooked (turn the steamed rice occasionally). Don't forget to put enough water in the steamer for steaming.

Tip: Serve this Nasi Kuning with Javanese chicken, ghudangan, potatoes fries-sambel and serundeng for a delicious meal.

MY NOTES

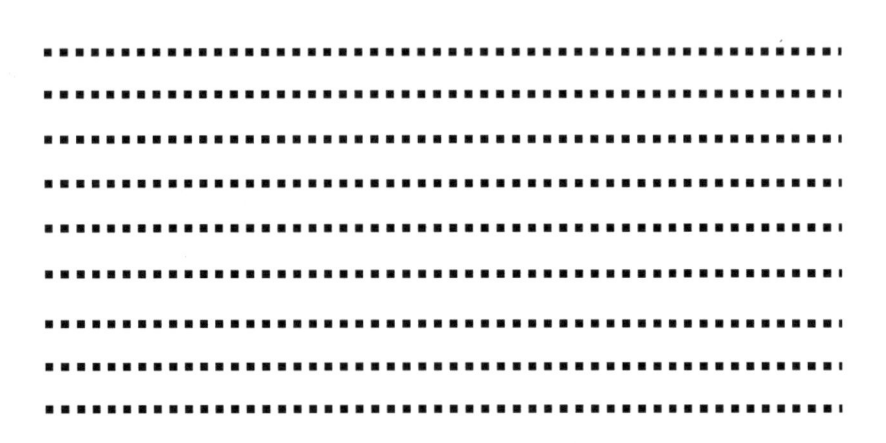

11. MASALA DUCK

Masala duck is a traditional Surinamese dish that is typically made with duck meat.
The dish is made by marinating the duck in a mixture of spices known as "masala" which is a blend of various herbs and spices such as cumin, coriander, turmeric, ginger, garlic, and chili peppers. The marinated duck is then cooked in a flavorful sauce, typically made with coconut milk, tomato, and various other spices.
The dish is often served with traditional Surinamese sides such as rice, roti (a type of flatbread), and various vegetables.

It is a popular dish in Suriname and the Netherlands, where Surinamese people live and is often served in Surinamese restaurants and homes.
It is quite spicy, and the flavor profile is a blend of sweet, sour, and spicy which is quite typical of Surinamese cuisine. The dish is also quite versatile as it can be served with different side dishes and vegetables.

It's a must-try for those who are interested in experiencing the rich and diverse flavors of Surinamese cuisine.

Ingredients:

- 1.5 kilograms of duck meat
- 2 onions, finely chopped
- 8 cloves of garlic, minced
- 3 tablespoons of masala spice blend
- 1 tomato, diced
- Black pepper, to taste
- 2 madame jeanette peppers, finely chopped
- 1 level tablespoon of cumin powder
- Oil
- Salt or Maggi cube, to taste

Note: Depending on the recipe, different ingredients might be used, but this list is a good starting point for a traditional Surinamese masala duck dish.

Instructions:

1. First, chop the duck into pieces and wash with lemon or vinegar.
2. Then chop the onions and tomato and set them aside. Mash the garlic and peppers to make a paste, using a mortar or a blender/chopper. In a cup, add a few drops of water and mix the masala with this to form a paste.
3. Now take a large pan and heat a layer of oil in it. About 6 to 7 tablespoons. Fry the onions and tomato in it and then add the garlic/pepper paste along with the masala. Fry this for a minute. Then add the duck. Mix it well with the ingredients. Add a pinch of black pepper and 2 Maggi cubes.
4. Put the lid on the pan and cook on medium heat to prevent burning. The meat should stew for at least an hour. After every 15 minutes, give it a quick stir. If you notice that the liquid dries out too much, add a little water. After half an hour, add the cumin powder.
5. After an hour, check if the meat is tender enough and then the duck is ready. If it is not tender enough, leave it for another 15 minutes. Taste it to see if it has enough salt, if not, add some more salt.

Tips:

- Masala can become bitter if you let it burn in the oil. So make sure this does not happen.
- Doks is more flavorful when it soaks in, so prepare it in the morning so it is deliciously absorbed before dinner. This is a nice change from roti with chicken.

MY NOTES

12. CASSAVA SOUP

Surinamese cassave soup is a traditional soup made with cassava, a root vegetable also known as yucca or manioc. The soup is typically made with a base of cassava, which is boiled and mashed, and then mixed with other ingredients such as onion, garlic, and spices such as cumin and pepper. The soup may also include meat or seafood, and is often served with rice or bread. It is a hearty and flavorful dish that is popular in Suriname and other parts of the Caribbean and South America.

Surinamese cassave soup is a popular creole dish that is easy to prepare. It is made with a base of boiled and mashed cassava, and can be flavored with a variety of meats such as salt meat, soup meat, chicken, or even vegetarian options. It is a hearty and flavorful soup that is enjoyed by many in Suriname.

Ingredients:

- 125 grams of salt meat
- 250 grams of soup meat (such as rib soup or poulet)
- 3 allspice grains
- 2 sprigs of celery (Surinamese soup vegetables)
- 8-10 pieces of cassava (can be frozen)
- 1 small can of coconut milk
- 1 onion, diced
- 1 tomato, diced
- 2 liters of water
- Bouillon cubes to taste (approximately 2 tablets)
- 1 Madam Jeanette pepper (a type of chili pepper)

Instructions:

To prepare Surinamese cassave soup, begin by boiling the salt meat and cutting it into cubes once it has been desalted. Next, gently boil the soup meat (such as rib soup or poulet) in a pressure cooker with a whole onion, a clove of garlic, and bouillon cubes to add flavor to the meat.

Take the frozen cassava pieces, thaw them slightly and cut them into cubes. Discard any strings that may be in the middle. Bring 2 liters of water to a boil and add diced onion, tomato, cassava, peppercorns, chopped celery, and 2 bouillon cubes. Cook for about 20 minutes.

After 20 minutes, check if the cassava has softened and add the meat and coconut milk. Continue cooking for an additional 20 minutes or until the cassava is fully cooked and the soup has thickened. While stirring, crush some of the cassava to thicken the soup.

For the last 10 minutes of cooking, add a Madam Jeanette pepper. Remove it after 10 minutes and taste the soup to adjust the seasoning if necessary.

Serve the soup in a bowl and with white rice on the side. Optional to add tayer leaf to the soup for more color. Instead of salt meat and soup meat, you can also use chicken breast or soup chicken and adjust the cooking time accordingly. Coconut milk is optional, it can be left out. You can use fresh cassava instead of frozen cassava.

MY NOTES

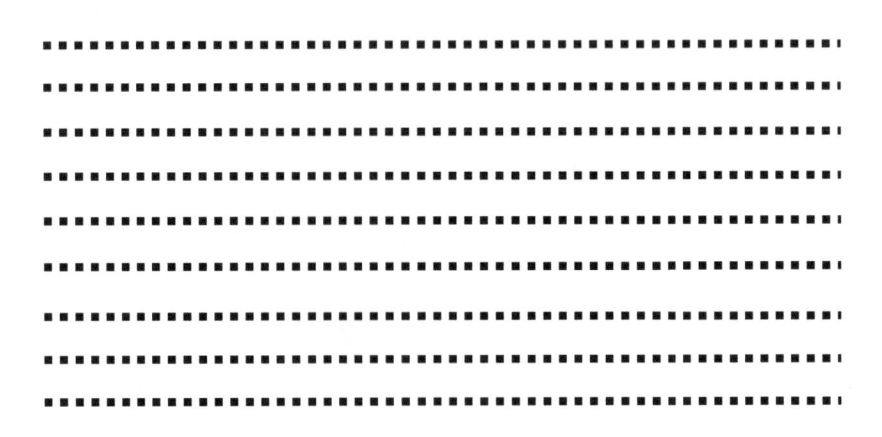

13. PEPRE WATRA (SURINAMESE FISH SOUP)

Pepre watra is a traditional Surinamese soup dish, typically made with freshly caught fish and served with homemade cassava bread. The origins of this dish can be traced back to Suriname, where it was often prepared by men after a day of fishing. In the past, smaller fish such as Kwie Kwie were used to make Pepre watra. The fish heads were not discarded, they were also used to make the soup.

This recipe is a simple and basic version of the dish. You can use different types of white fish such as pike or cod to make the soup. The preparation method may vary depending on the type of fish used. It is a hearty and flavorful dish that is enjoyed by many in Suriname and other parts of the Caribbean and South America.

Ingredients:

- 2 liters of water
- 500 grams of white fish including the head (such as pike or headless cod fillet)
- 5 allspice grains
- 3 sprigs of celery
- 1 onion, diced
- 1 Madam Jeanette pepper (a type of chili pepper)
- Salt to taste
- 2 bouillon cubes
- 1 teaspoon of black pepper
- 1 tomato, diced
- 1 lemon, juiced
- Cassava bread (bakka kassaba) for serving

Instructions:

To prepare Pepre watra, begin by cleaning and preparing the fish. Remove the intestines and scales, and if using a whole fish, cut it into pieces. Wash the fish with lemon juice and sprinkle salt and black pepper over it and set it aside.

In a large soup pot, bring 2 liters of water to a boil with 2 bouillon cubes, 1 diced onion, 6 allspice grains, finely chopped celery, and diced tomato. Let it cook for about 10 minutes.

After 10 minutes, add the fish and the Madam Jeanette pepper (whole) to the pot, cover it with a lid, and let it cook for 30 minutes on medium heat.

After 30 minutes, taste the soup and adjust the seasoning if necessary. If the soup is too spicy, remove the Madam Jeanette pepper.

The soup is ready and it's served with cassava bread. You break off a piece of cassava bread and dip it into your soup to make it soft! You can also serve it with a small bowl of rice if desired.

Tips:
- The more pepper you use the hotter your soup. You can also have 2 peppers in the soup.
- If you want more vegetables in the soup, you can add finely chopped leeks or carrots.
- Cassava bread is usually eaten with pepre watra but some people do not like it. Ladle the soup and then serve it with a small bowl of rice.

MY NOTES

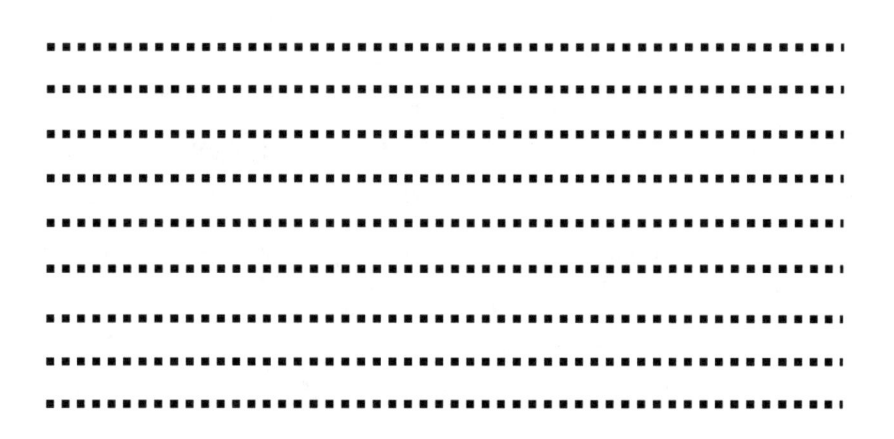

14. PEANUT SOUP

Surinamese peanut soup, also known as "pindasoep," is a traditional soup made with peanuts as the main ingredient. The soup is typically made by grinding roasted peanuts into a paste, which is then mixed with other ingredients such as onion, garlic, and spices such as cumin and pepper.

The soup may also include meat such as chicken or beef, and vegetables such as carrots, sweet potatoes, or spinach. It is a hearty and flavorful dish that is popular in Suriname and other parts of the Caribbean and South America.

The soup is usually served with rice or bread. The peanut paste gives the soup a creamy texture, and it can also be served as a thicker stew. Some variations of the soup also include coconut milk, which gives the soup a richer flavor.

Ingredients:

- 1.5 liters of water
- 1 jar (350 grams) of peanut butter (such as Calve brand)
- 2 sprigs of celery
- 200 grams of salt meat
- 1 piece of pork tail (aggutere)
- 500 grams of chicken (such as legs or thighs)
- 5 allspice grains (lontai)
- 2 bay leaves
- 2-3 bouillon cubes
- 1 large onion, diced
- 1 tomato, diced
- 2 tablespoons of oil

These ingredients will be used to make the soup. Peanut butter is the main ingredient and it will be mixed with other ingredients such as onion, tomato, celery, allspice, bay leaves, bouillon cubes, and oil. The soup will also include meats such as salt meat, pork tail and chicken. It is a hearty and flavorful dish that is popular in Suriname and other parts of the Caribbean and South America.

Instructions:

To prepare Surinamese peanut soup, begin by boiling the salt meat and pork tail until they are tender and then draining them. Cut the salt meat into cubes and the pork tail into pieces. Wash the chicken and set it aside.

In a large soup pot, heat some oil and fry the onion and tomato. Then add the chicken, salt pork, and pork tail and cook for 5 minutes on medium heat. Deglaze the pot with water, and then add allspice grains, bay leaves, 1 sprig of chopped celery, and 2 bouillon cubes. Let it boil for about 40 minutes on low heat.

After 40 minutes of cooking, ladle some of the broth into a separate pot without the meats. Mix in the peanut butter and broth, making sure it dissolves completely. Remove the chicken from the pot, trying to remove as much of the bone as possible. Pour the dissolved peanut butter back into the soup pot and let it cook for another 10 minutes. Taste the soup and adjust the seasoning if necessary.

When the soup is ready, add pepper and the last sprig of celery. Do not break the pepper, as it releases its aroma when left whole. Serve the soup with rice and tom tom.

Tips:
- Replace 75 grams of regular peanut butter with Faja lobi peanut cheese once for a spicy soup

MY NOTES

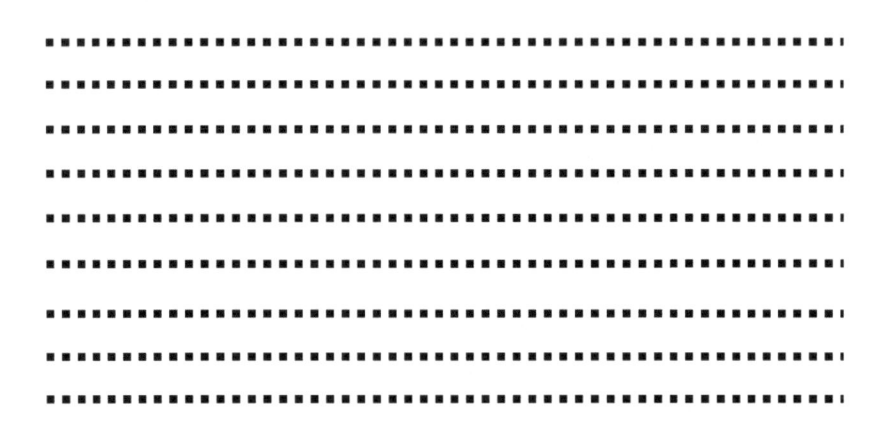

....
....
....
....
....
....
....
....
....

15. HERI HERI

Heri heri is a traditional Surinamese one-pot dish that has a rich history rooted in the country's past. The name "heri heri" literally translates to "whole whole" or "heal heal," but it can also refer to the fact that it is a one-pot dish.

The origins of heri heri can be traced back to the time of slavery in Suriname. It was a dish that was consumed by slaves to provide them with the necessary energy to work for long hours. In those days, they often ate only once a day and had to make do with whatever ingredients were available. The dish was typically made with banana, cassava, and sweet potato, and if salted fish was available, it would be added to the dish. Over time, other ingredients such as egg and vegetables were added to the dish.

During the time of slavery, heri heri was considered a "power food," as it kept the slaves going through difficult times. Nowadays, the dish has become a festive dish celebrated during important occasions, such as the national holiday of Keti Koti, which marks the abolition of slavery in Suriname. Eating the dish and knowing its history is a way to keep the past from being forgotten.

Ingredients:

- 2 bags (450 grams each) of cod fish
- 3 shallots or onions
- 4 cloves of garlic
- 1 small cassava (about 500 grams)
- 650 grams of orange sweet potato
- 350 grams of white sweet potato
- 2 green plantains
- 1 ripe brown plantain
- 3 Chinese tayer or taro tubers
- 300 grams of long beans
- 6 eggs
- Sunflower oil
- Coconut oil
- 1 tablespoon of tomato paste
- 1 large vine tomato or 2 small vine tomatoes, diced
- Black pepper

Instructions:

To prepare Surinamese Heri Heri, you will need to start by pre-rinsing and boiling the bakkeljauw (salted and dried cod) to remove the excess salt. Then, you will need to chop the shallot and garlic, and cut and wash all the other vegetables and fruits, including the cassava, sweet potatoes, plantains and Chinese tayer.

Cook the vegetables and fruits in stages, starting with the cassava for 7 minutes, then adding the rest of the vegetables and cooking for an additional 15 minutes. Drain and peel the plantains, and boil the eggs. While the vegetables are cooking, you can prepare the bakkeljauw and long beans by frying them in a pan with shallot, garlic, tomato paste and vine tomatoes.

Once everything is cooked, you can start preparing the plates by placing a generous amount of cooked vegetables and fruits, a halved egg, a scoop of long beans and bakkeljauw on each plate. Serve with sambal as desired.

MY NOTES

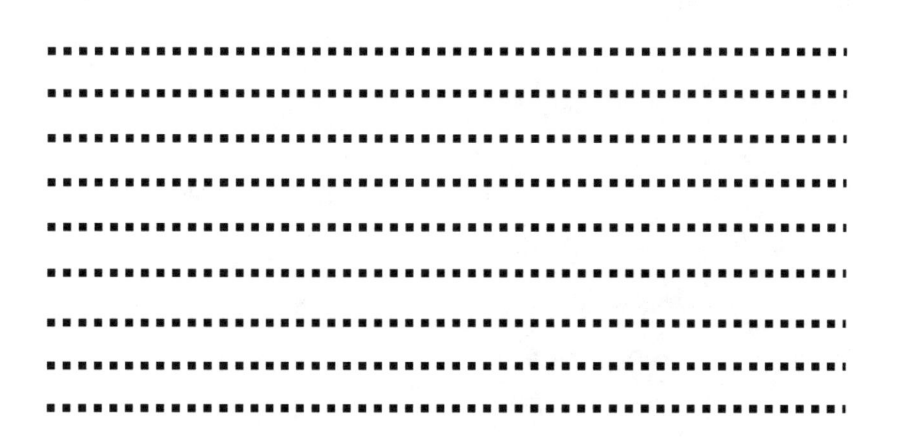

16. BARA

Bara is a traditional Surinamese food that is a type of fried dumpling made from a combination of ground split peas, flour, and spices. The dough is shaped into small rounds and then deep-fried until golden brown. It is often served as a snack or as an accompaniment to a main dish.

The main ingredient in Bara is ground split peas, which are also known as yellow split peas. These are soaked overnight and then ground into a fine paste. The paste is then combined with flour, baking powder, salt, and spices such as cumin, coriander, and turmeric. Some variations may also include grated onion, garlic, or chilies.
Bara is usually served with a variety of toppings and condiments, including tamarind sauce, chutney, and a spicy pepper sauce. Some people also like to serve it with a side of curried vegetables or a salad.

The origins of Bara are believed to be from the Indian subcontinent, brought over to Suriname by indentured laborers during the colonial period. It has since become a staple in Surinamese cuisine and can be found in many street vendors and restaurants.

Ingredients:

- 750 grams of wheat flour
- 300 grams of finely ground urdi (mung beans)
- 6 crushed cloves of garlic
- 6 tajer leaves (preferably young)
- 1 teaspoon baking soda
- 1 teaspoon baking powder
- 1½ teaspoon salt
- 2 teaspoons massala
- 2 teaspoons ground djira (cumin seeds or cumin powder)
- ½ pepper (madame jeanette without seeds)
- 1 liter sunflower oil
- water

To make the dough for the Bara, combine the wheat flour, ground urdi, crushed garlic, finely chopped tajer leaves, baking soda, baking powder, salt, massala, ground djira and pepper in a large mixing bowl. Gradually mix in enough water to form a smooth and slightly sticky dough.

Cover the dough and let it rest for about 30 minutes to allow the flavors to develop. After the dough has rested, divide it into small balls about the size of a golf ball. Flatten each ball into a disk shape and press a small indentation in the center of each disk.

In a deep pan or pot, heat the sunflower oil over medium-high heat. When the oil is hot, gently drop in the Bara discs, being careful not to overcrowd the pan. Fry the Bara until they are golden brown and crispy, flipping them occasionally. Drain them on a paper towel-lined plate to remove excess oil.

The Bara can be served with a variety of toppings and condiments, including tamarind sauce, chutney, and a spicy pepper sauce. Enjoy it as a snack or as an accompaniment to a main dish.

Instructions:

1. In a large bowl, mix together the wheat flour, urdi, garlic, tajer leaves, baking soda, baking powder, salt, massala, djira, and pepper.
2. Slowly add water to the mixture until you have a thick batter that is easy to handle.
3. Heat the sunflower oil in a deep pan or wok until it reaches 350-375°F (175-190°C).
4. Take a spoonful of the batter and drop it into the hot oil. Repeat this process until the pan is full, but not overcrowded.
5. Fry the bara's for about 2-3 minutes on each side or until golden brown.
6. Remove the bara's from the oil with a slotted spoon and place them on a plate lined with paper towels to absorb any excess oil.
7. Serve the bara's hot with a side of chutney, sambal, or other dipping sauce.

Note: You can add some chopped onions, finely chopped chives or cilantro to the batter to give it some extra flavor. Also, you can use a combination of wheat flour and corn flour to make the bara's more crispy.

MY NOTES

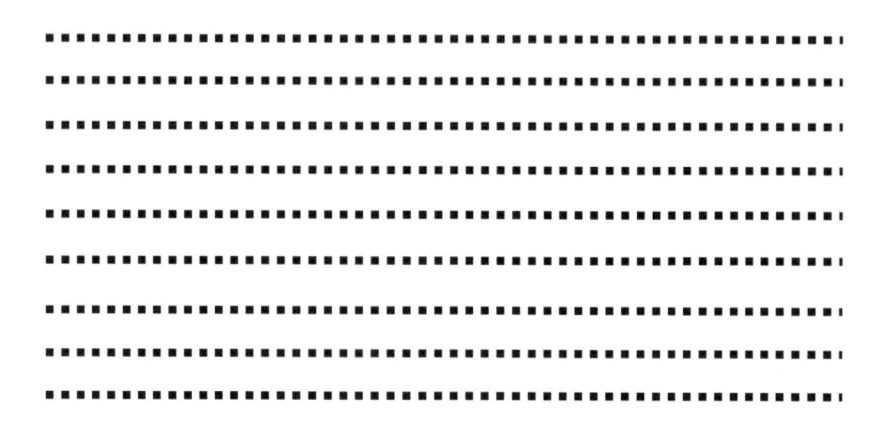

17. GUDANGAN

Gudangan, also spelled Goedangan, is a traditional Javanese dish from Indonesia. It typically consists of a combination of fresh vegetables, such as cucumber, tomato, and long beans, which are cooked with pepper and coconut.

The vegetables are usually sliced or diced and then stir-fried with spices, such as shallots, garlic, and chili, and grated coconut. The dish is known for its fresh and light flavors, as well as its simple and quick preparation.

Gudangan is often served as a side dish, but it can also be enjoyed as a main meal. It is particularly popular during hot weather, as the fresh vegetables and coconut provide a refreshing and cooling effect.

The dish is also quite versatile, and variations can include adding meat, seafood, or tofu, and adjusting the level of spiciness to taste.

Traditionally, Gudangan is served with steamed rice and other side dishes, such as sambal, a chili-based condiment, and a type of meat or fish dish. It's a staple in Javanese cuisine and is easy to find in most Indonesian restaurants.

Ingredients:

- 200 grams of bean sprouts
- ½ pound cabbage
- ½ pound long beans
- ½ pound claroon or dagu leaf
- ½ teaspoon salt
- water
- grated coconut
- sambal
- peanut sauce
- 2 boiled eggs

Instructions:

To prepare, begin by washing and cutting all the vegetables. Clean the bean sprouts by removing the brown ends and trim the ends off of the long beans before cutting them into 2cm pieces. Cut the cabbage and chives, but not too finely.

Bring a pan of water to a boil and add salt. Cook the vegetables one by one, starting with the long beans and finishing with the leafy greens. Drain the vegetables well.

Make a tasty satay sauce, then arrange the vegetables on a plate. Garnish with coconut bubbles, a boiled egg, and satay sauce. Add fried onions as desired.

To make coconut sambal, mix grated coconut with garlic, pepper, kentjoor, trasie, sugar, and salt to taste. Fry in a pan until dry.

MY NOTES

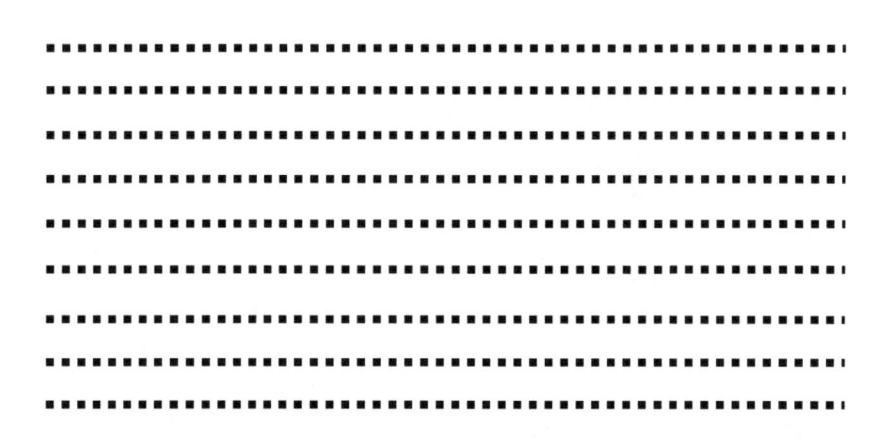

18. PITJEL

Pitjel is a traditional Surinamese-Javanese dish that features a variety of vegetables cooked to perfection and served with a spicy peanut sauce. The dish is known for its colorful presentation, with a variety of vegetables including water spinach, bean sprouts, long beans, and cabbage.

The vegetables are usually cooked al dente and served warm or cold, making it a popular salad-like dish. Pitjel is often served with white rice, and is considered a fusion of Surinamese and Indonesian cuisines.

The dish is a local version of the Javanese dish pecel, and is similar to the Indonesian dish gadogado. The dish was introduced to Suriname by Indonesian contract workers brought to the country in the late 19th century to work on the plantations, and has since been adapted to have a distinct Surinamese flavor.

Ingredients:

- 250 grams of long beans
- 250 grams of bean sprouts
- 1 small white cabbage (400 grams)
- 1 bunch of dagou leaves
- peanut sauce
- salt

Instructions:

1. Start by washing and chopping the long beans and pointed cabbage. Cut them into strands.
2. Cook the long beans and pointed cabbage until they are al dente, or have a crunchy bite.
3. After 15 minutes of cooking, add the bean sprouts (with the brown strings removed) and cook for an additional 2 minutes.
4. While the vegetables are cooking, prepare the peanut sauce, or satay sauce, to be poured over the dish later.
5. Once the vegetables are cooked, place them on a plate and pour the prepared peanut sauce over them.
6. Enjoy your homemade Pitjel and savor the unique flavors of this traditional Surinamese-Javanese dish.

MY NOTES

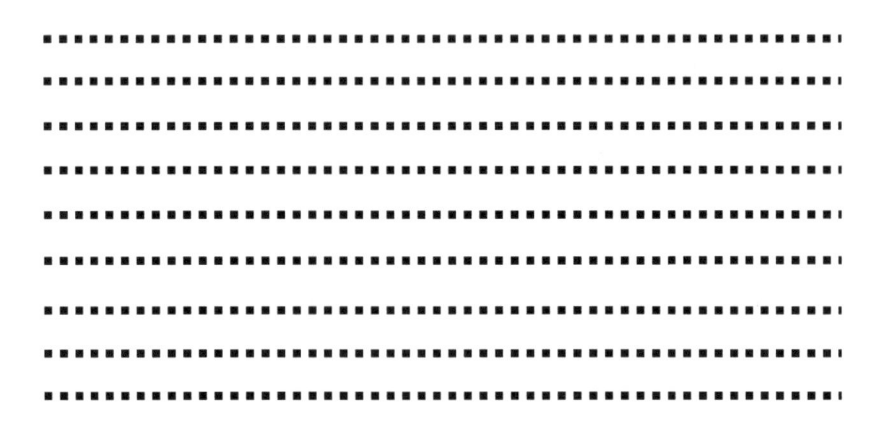

19. OKER SOUP OKRO BRAVOE

Surinamese oker soup, also known as Okro Bravoe, is a traditional dish from Suriname, a country in South America that was a Dutch colony until 1975. The dish is a hearty soup made with oker, which is a type of leafy green vegetable that is native to Suriname and is also known as "callaloo" or "spinach bush". It is a staple in the Surinamese cuisine, and it is a popular dish that is enjoyed by many.

The oker leaves are typically cooked with ingredients such as coconut milk, onions, garlic, ginger, and a variety of spices, including cumin, coriander, and turmeric. The soup is typically made with some type of meat or fish, such as chicken, beef, or prawns. Some recipes may include additional vegetables such as okra, pumpkin, or tomato. The soup is known for its thick, creamy texture and rich, flavorful taste.

Okro Bravoe is a popular dish in Suriname and is often served as a main course, usually with rice. It is considered a comfort food and is often enjoyed during the rainy season. The soup is considered a healthy and nutritious dish that is also rich in vitamins and minerals. The oker soup is also considered a fusion of Surinamese, African, and Indian cuisine as the ingredients used in the soup are a combination of these cultures. The African slaves who were brought to Suriname during the colonial era brought the tradition of making a soup with leafy greens and the Indian coolies who came as contract workers during the 19th century brought the use of coconut milk and spices in the dish.

Okro Bravoe is also famous for being a popular street food in Suriname and is usually sold by street vendors, it's also served in many restaurants throughout the country. The dish is considered a comfort food and is enjoyed by people of all ages.

Ingredients:

- 250 grams of soup chicken
- 150 grains of salt meat (cooked and cut into pieces about 1.5×1.5 cm)
- 2 liters of water (keep 1 extra liter of water aside)
- 4 small antroea
- 4 peppercorns
- 1 madam jeanette pepper
- 4 sprigs of celery
- 10 ochers
- 1 onion
- 1 bunch of tajer leaf (about 8 sprigs)
- 2 vegetable stock cubes rice for 4 persons

Instructions:

1. Begin by washing and boiling the salt meat, then cut it into 1.5 cm cubes. Clean the chicken by washing it with vinegar or lemon, and cut it into larger pieces of about 4 cm. Cut the onions into rings and the celery into coarse pieces. Peel the ochers by grating the outside with a knife and removing the top, then slice them. Remove the stem and wash the tajer leaves well.
2. In a large saucepan, bring 2 liters of water to a boil. Add 4 allspice grains, the soup vegetables, onions, 2 bouillon cubes, and the tager leaf. Allow this to boil for about 15 minutes. Take out the tajer leaf and set it aside in a separate bowl or pan. Add the chicken, salt pork, ochers, and antroeas to the soup pan and cook on medium-low heat for about 20 minutes.
3. Finely beat the tajer leaf that was set aside and add it back to the soup. This will give the soup a thicker texture. Taste the soup and add salt as needed. If the soup is too thick, add a little water. If it's too thin, remove the lid for the last 10 minutes to allow the water to evaporate. Do not let the pepper burst open, as this will make the soup too hot.
4. Serve the rice on a flat plate and the soup in a deep bowl. Make sure to provide one antroea per serving. Let your diners know that there are allspice grains in the soup. If desired, remove the allspice grains at the end of the cooking time so guests won't find them in their soup.

MY NOTES

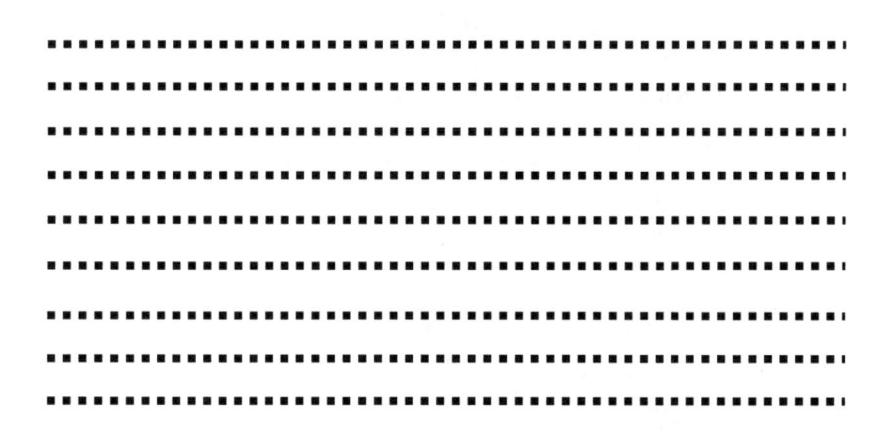

....
....
....
....
....
....
....
....
....

20. STIR-FRIED TAHOE

Tofu or Tahoe, is a traditional Asian food made from soybeans. The process of making tofu involves extracting soy milk from ground soybeans, and then curdling the milk with a coagulant, such as nigari (magnesium chloride) or gypsum (calcium sulfate). The curds are then pressed into blocks and cooled, resulting in tofu. Tofu is a versatile food that can be used in a variety of dishes, from soups and stews to stir-fries and salads. It is also a popular meat substitute for vegetarians and vegans.

Tofu comes in different varieties, depending on the firmness, texture, and flavor. The most common types include silken, soft, medium, and firm tofu. Silken tofu is the most delicate and has the highest water content, making it ideal for smoothies, dips, and dressings. Soft tofu is slightly firmer and is ideal for soups and stews. Medium and firm tofu are best for stir-fries, grilling, and deep-frying.

Tofu can be prepared in a variety of ways, such as marinating, sautéing, grilling, or deep-frying. It can also be used as an ingredient in many different dishes such as soups, stir-fries, salads, and sandwiches. Tofu can also be flavored with different spices, sauces, and marinades to enhance its taste.

In general, Tofu is a healthy and versatile food that can be used in a variety of dishes and can be a good source of protein for vegetarians and vegans. It is low in calories, cholesterol-free, and contains a variety of vitamins and minerals. Tofu can be prepared in many different ways and can be flavored to enhance its taste.

Ingredients:

- 750 grams firm tofu
- 3 tbsp sunflower oil
- 1 tbsp pressed garlic
- 1 tbsp grated ginger
- 2 dried chili peppers
- 2 spring onions, chopped
- 80 ml water
- 2 tbsp soy sauce
- 1 tbsp toasted sesame seeds

Instructions:

1. Cut the tofu into 1.5 cm cubes and pat dry. Cut the chili pepper into small pieces and remove the seeds. Finely chop the spring onion and separate the white part from the green part.
2. Heat a wok with 3 tablespoons of oil. Stir-fry the pressed garlic, ginger, and chili pepper for 15 seconds over high heat. Then add the tofu and white part of the spring onions. Stir-fry for a few minutes until lightly browned.
3. Add 80 ml of water and ¼ teaspoon of salt. Stir and let half of the liquid evaporate. Once this is done, add the green part of the spring onion and the soy sauce. Stir well and taste, adding more salt if needed. Garnish with the toasted sesame seeds.

Tips: Try experimenting with different vegetables such as long beans or you can also choose to make stuffed tofu.

MY NOTES

21. LONG BEANS WITH SALT MEAT

Surinamese Long beans with salt meat is a traditional dish from Suriname. The dish typically consists of long beans (also known as yard-long beans or Chinese long beans) that are stir-fried with salt meat, which is typically a type of cured pork.

The long beans are usually sliced into thin, 2-3 inches long pieces, and stir-fried with diced salt meat, onions, and garlic. Spices such as cumin, black pepper, and coriander, and sometimes curry powder, are added to the dish to give it a unique flavor. The dish is usually served with rice and can also be served with chicken or fish.

In Suriname, this dish is traditionally served as a part of a larger spread of food, typically served with other side dishes such as roti, dhal, and achar. It is a popular and hearty dish that is often enjoyed at family gatherings and special occasions.

In summary, Surinamese Long beans with salt meat is a traditional dish from Suriname which consist of long beans stir-fried with salt meat, onions, and garlic and typically served with rice. The dish is characterized by its unique blend of spices and strong flavors, and is often served as part of a larger spread of food.

Ingredients:

- 400 grams long beans, sliced into thin 2-3 inches pieces
- 200 grams salt meat, diced
- 1 onion, finely chopped
- 1 garlic clove, pressed
- 2 tsp tomato paste
- pinch of white pepper
- 1 tsp herb broth powder (or 1-2 Maggi cubes)
- 2-3 tbsp sunflower oil
- 1/2 cup water

Instructions:

1. Begin by washing the long beans and cutting off the tops. Then, cut the long beans into pieces about 3cm long. Soak the salt meat in water for about 30 minutes to soften it, then dice the meat.
2. Heat a pan with oil and fry the onion and garlic. After a minute, add the tomato paste and salted meat. Stir-fry until the meat is slightly crispy.
3. Add the long beans, herb broth powder, and white pepper to the pan. Mix well with the vegetables.
4. Add 1/2 cup of water, cover the pan and cook for about 10 minutes on medium-high heat. Make sure to stir occasionally to prevent burning.
5. Remove the lid for the last 3 minutes of cooking to allow the excess water to evaporate.

Tips: This vegetable dish is typically served with rice. It can also be delicious on a white roll or Surinamese rolls. If you don't eat meat, you can also prepare long beans with shrimp or salmon for a tasty alternative.

MY NOTES

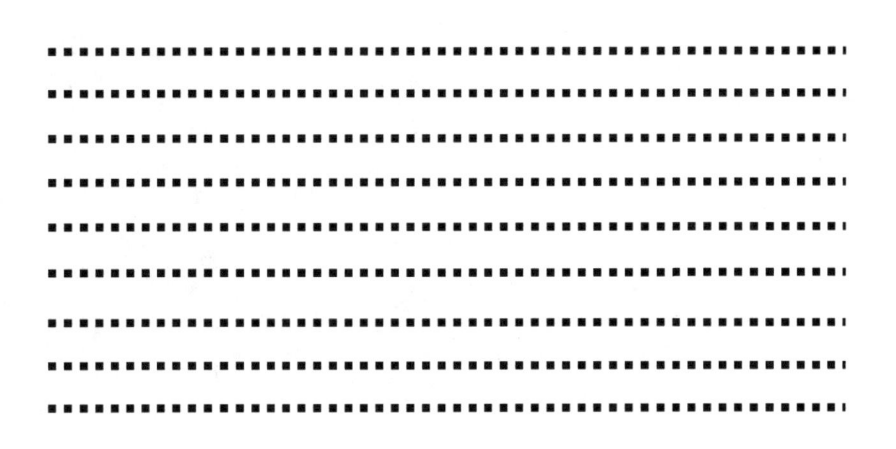

22.PRAWNS WITH COCONUT MILK

Surinamese Prawns with Coconut Milk is a traditional dish from Suriname. The dish typically consists of prawns that are cooked in a flavorful sauce made with coconut milk, spices and herbs.

The prawns are usually cleaned and deveined before being cooked in the sauce. The sauce is made by sautéing onions, garlic, and ginger in oil, then adding spices such as cumin, turmeric, coriander, and curry powder. Tomato paste, and coconut milk are also added to the sauce to give it a creamy and rich texture. The prawns are then simmered in the sauce until they are cooked through.

This dish is typically served with rice, and is considered a hearty and comforting meal. The coconut milk provides a rich and creamy base for the dish, and the spices and herbs give it a unique and complex flavor. The prawns are a good source of protein and provide a meaty texture to the dish.

In summary, Surinamese Prawns with Coconut Milk is a traditional dish from Suriname, which consists of prawns cooked in a flavorful sauce made with coconut milk, spices and herbs. This dish is typically served with rice and is considered a hearty and comforting meal. The coconut milk provides a rich and creamy base, the spices and herbs give a unique and complex flavor and prawns as a good source of protein.

Ingredients:

- 250 grams Gambas (prawns)
- 1 bell pepper, diced
- 1 cup coconut milk
- 1 salam leaf (Indonesian bay leaf)
- 2 cloves garlic, minced
- 1 onion, shredded
- 4 tbsp oil
- pinch of black pepper
- 1 Maggi cube
- 1 tomato, diced
- 1 Madame Jeanette pepper (a type of chili pepper)

Instructions:

1. Clean and devein the Gambas.
2. In a pan, heat oil and sauté onion, garlic and ginger until translucent.
3. Add the diced bell pepper, diced tomato, Madame Jeanette pepper, and spices (cumin, turmeric, coriander, curry powder, black pepper and maggi cube) and stir-fry for a few minutes.
4. Add the coconut milk and salam leaf.
5. Add the Gambas, and let it simmer for a few minutes or until the prawns are cooked through.
6. Serve it hot with rice

Tips: Try using different types of seafood such as fish or scallops. Adjust the amount of Madame Jeanette pepper to your taste preference. You can also add some vegetables like carrots or okra for a more nutritious dish.

The Surinamese Cookbook is a comprehensive guide to the traditional and contemporary cuisine of Suriname. With 22 delicious and authentic recipes, this cookbook provides an excellent opportunity for anyone to experience the rich and diverse flavors of Surinamese food. Whether you're a seasoned cook or just starting out, the recipes in this book are designed to be simple and quick to prepare, making them perfect for busy weeknights.

The ingredients used in the recipes are widely available, making it easy to recreate the dishes at home. Whether you're looking for a flavorful and aromatic main course, a delicious side dish, or a sweet and satisfying dessert, the Surinamese Cookbook has something to offer.

In addition to the recipes, the Surinamese Cookbook also provides a glimpse into the culture and history of Suriname, making it a valuable resource for anyone interested in learning more about this fascinating country. The recipes are accompanied by short descriptions of the dishes' origins and cultural significance, giving readers a deeper appreciation of the food and the people who create it.

In conclusion, the Surinamese Cookbook is a must-have for anyone looking to expand their cooking repertoire and bring the flavors of Suriname into their home. With its simple, quick-to-prepare recipes and beautiful photography, this cookbook is an excellent resource for anyone looking to impress their loved ones with the delicious and authentic tastes of Surinamese cuisine.

Made in the USA
Columbia, SC
08 May 2025